Pteranodon

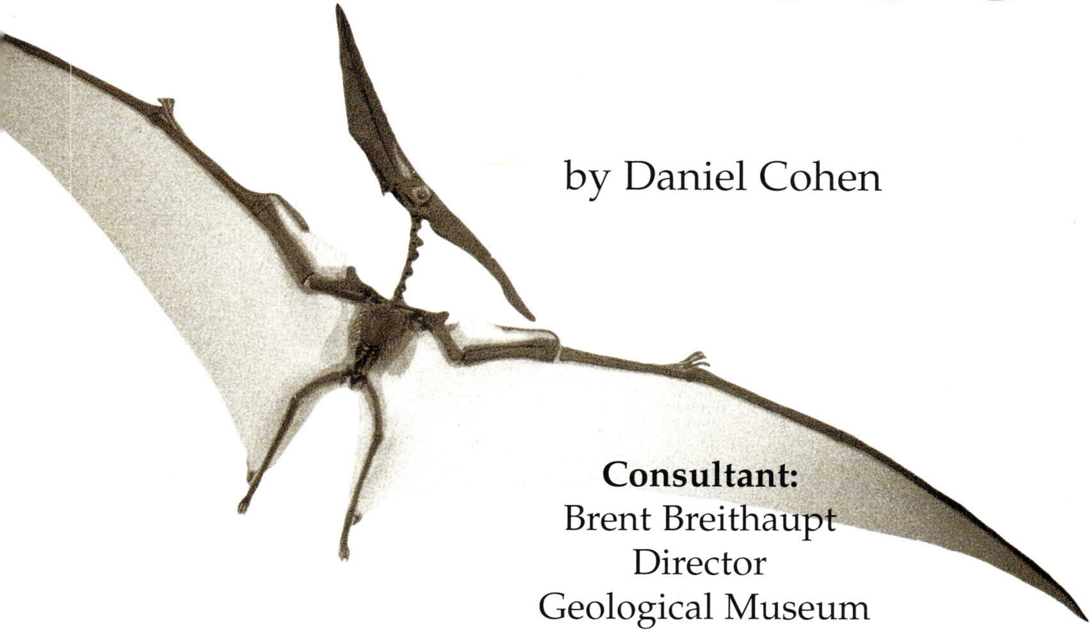

by Daniel Cohen

Consultant:
Brent Breithaupt
Director
Geological Museum
University of Wyoming

Bridgestone Books
an imprint of Capstone Press
Mankato, Minnesota

Bridgestone Books are published by Capstone Press
151 Good Counsel Drive, P.O. Box 669, Mankato, Minnesota 56002
http://www.capstone-press.com

Library of Congress Cataloging-in-Publication Data
Cohen, Daniel, 1936–
    Pteranodon/by Daniel Cohen.
    p. cm.—(The Bridgestone Science Library)
    Includes bibliographical references and index.
    Summary: Discusses the physical characteristics, habitat, food, relatives, and extinction of
this flying reptile that lived on the Earth during the Age of Dinosaurs.
    ISBN 0-7368-0617-2
    1. Pteranodon—Juvenile literature. [1. Pteranodon. 2. Prehistoric animals.] I. Title.
    II. Series.
QE862.P7 C64 2001
567.918—dc21
            00-021733

Editorial Credits
Erika Mikkelson, editor; Linda Clavel, cover designer and illustrator; Heidi Schoof
  and Kimberly Danger, photo researchers

Photo Credits
David F. Clobes, 16–17
Index Stock Imagery, 6–7
James P. Rowan, 12
Kent and Donna Dannen, 8, 20
Unicorn Stock Photos/Doug Adams, 14
Visuals Unlimited/John D. Cunningham, cover, 1; Ken Lucas, 4; A. J. Copley, 10–11

1 2 3 4 5 6 06 05 04 03 02 01

Table of Contents

Pteranodon compared to a 5-foot-tall
(1.5-meter-tall) human

Pteranodon

The name Pteranodon (terr-AN-oh-don) means winged and toothless. Pteranodon was a winged reptile. It lived more than 65 million years ago. Dinosaurs lived during the time of Pteranodon.

reptile
a cold-blooded animal with a backbone

The Pteranodon's World

The earth looked different 65 million years ago. The climate was warm and wet. Giant ferns, gingkos, and other plants covered the land.

climate
the usual weather in a place

This winged reptile is Quetzalcoatlus. Quetzalcoatlus and Pteranodon were pterosaurs.

Relatives of Pteranodon

Pteranodon belonged to a group of winged reptiles called pterosaurs (terr-oh-SORES). Some pterosaurs had a wingspan of only 10 inches (25 centimeters). The largest pterosaur had a wingspan of 39 feet (12 meters). These pterosaurs were the largest flying creatures to ever live on Earth.

wingspan
the distance between the outer tips of an animal's wings

beak

crest

claws

wing

legs

claws

wing

Parts of Pteranodon

Pteranodon was one of the largest pterosaurs. Pteranodon had a wingspan of up to 30 feet (9 meters). Thin leathery skin covered its body and wings. Pteranodon had a large toothless beak and a flat bony crest. It had two thin legs and two small feet.

crest
a flat bony plate on top of Pteranodon's head

11

What Pteranodon Ate

Most scientists believe Pteranodon ate
fish. Pteranodon lived near oceans and
lakes. The animal flew above the
surface of the water. It may have
scooped up fish with its long beak.
Today, some sea birds catch fish the
same way.

Predators of Pteranodon

Pteranodon was smaller than many dinosaurs. It weighed about 37 pounds (17 kilograms). Large meat-eating dinosaurs such as Tyrannosaurus rex may have attacked Pteranodon. It protected itself by flying high above its predators.

predator
an animal that hunts and eats other animals

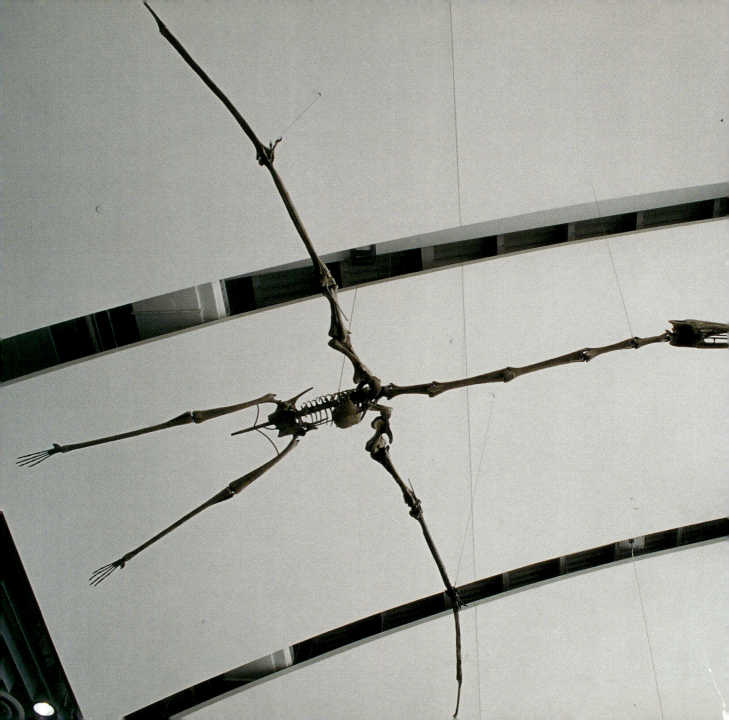

Pterosaur bones help scientists learn more about how pterosaurs became extinct.

The End of Pteranodon

Pteranodon and other pterosaurs became extinct about 65 million years ago. All dinosaurs also died at this time. Scientists do not know why these animals became extinct.

extinct
no longer living anywhere in the world

17

UNITED STATES

Wyoming

South Dakota

Kansas

States where Pteranodon fossils have been found

Discovering Pteranodon

In 1870, a group of paleontologists led by Othniel Charles Marsh discovered Pteranodon fossils in Kansas. In 1876, Marsh named the fossils Pteranodon.

fossils
the remains or traces of something that once lived

Studying Pteranodon Today

Paleontologists continue to discover and study fossils of Pteranodon and its relatives. New discoveries and research show that Pteranodon flapped its wings to fly. Paleontologists know that Pteranodon was one of the first animals with a backbone to fly.

Hands On: The Wingspan of Pteranodon

Pterosaurs were the largest flying creatures to ever live on Earth. Pteranodon was among the largest of the pterosaurs. You can see how large its wingspan was in this activity.

What You Need

Tape measure
At least 10 friends

What You Do

1. One person stands with his or her arms straight out from his or her side.
2. Another person measures the length of the person's outstretched arms. Measure from the tip of the left middle finger to the tip of the right middle finger.
3. Repeat steps one and two with another person. The second person should stand next to the first person. Their fingertips should touch.
4. Continue to add people until the total length of their outstretched arms is about 30 feet (9 meters). How many people did it take to equal the wingspan of one Pteranodon?

Words to Know

dinosaur (DYE-na-sore)—an extinct land reptile; dinosaurs lived on Earth for more than 150 million years.

extinct (ek-STINGKT)—no longer living anywhere in the world; dinosaurs and pterosaurs became extinct 65 million years ago.

gingko (GING-koh)—a tree with green fan-shaped leaves

paleontologist (PAY-lee-on-TOL-ah-jist)—a scientist who finds and studies fossils

reptile (REP-tile)—a cold-blooded animal with a backbone; scales cover a reptile's body.

scientist (SYE-uhn-tist)—a person who studies the world around us

Read More

Fisher, Enid. *True Life Monsters of the Prehistoric Skies.* World of Dinosaurs. Milwaukee: Gareth Stevens, 1999.

Rodriguez, K. S. *Pteranodon.* Prehistoric Creatures Then and Now. Austin, Texas: Steadwell Books, 2000.

Internet Sites

Blast from the Past
http://www.nmnh.si.edu/paleo/blast

Pteranodon
http://www.enchantedlearning.com/subjects/
dinosaurs/dinos/Pteranodon.shtml

A Pteranodon Dig
http://www.oceansofkansas.com/page5.html

Pterosauria
http://www.ucmp.berkeley.edu/diapsids/pterosauria.html

Index

$18.60

DATE			